FLOUT

Stephanie Green

HappenStance

ISBN 978-1-910131-12-1

Acknowledgements:
Thanks to editors of the following magazines in which some of these poems were previously published: *Edinburgh Review 130, Glasgow Review, Northwords Now, The New Shetlander* and *Southlight 15.* 'First Long Walk after Convalescence' was long-listed in the Strokestown (Ireland) Poetry competition, 2012.

'The Child of Breckon Sands' was set to music for voice and piano by Marisa Sharon Hartanto on the Young Composers' course and performed by the mezzo-soprano Alison Wells at the St Magnus Festival, Orkney, 2013.

Many thanks to Patricia Ace, Gill Andrews, Vicki Feaver, John Glenday, Jane McKie and Kona Macphee for editorial suggestions. Special thanks to Jen Hadfield and, for her support over the years, to Liz Lochhead.

The author gratefully acknowledges the support of the National Lottery through the Scottish Arts Council by giving her a New Writers' Bursary in 2007 and Creative Scotland for two further grants in 2010 and 2011 towards spending time in Shetland to enable the writing of this title.

Poetry by the same author:
Glass Works, Cat's Pyjamas Publications, 2005

Printed by The Dolphin Press
www.dolphinpress.co.uk

Published in 2015 by Happen*Stance,*
21 Hatton Green, Glenrothes, Fife KY7 4SD
nell@happenstancepress.com
www.happenstancepress.com

CONTENTS

for
Mark and James

ADOLESCENT

Bursting out of his feathers,
all shoulders and claws,

a ball of squawks,
fluff and no style.

His neck jerks up,
shuts like a telescope.

A shrug and high dudgeon,
he sulks and *hurrumps*.

Now up in the air,
he leans against the wind,

describes an elegant arc
against the sky.

THE WIND'S RANT: A FIDDLERS' SET

i. Jen's Delight

Laurie is birling down the bus
round the poles, right, left and off.
What's got into her?

The wind coughs, like a grumpy skorie
                who huff puffs,
then back-swerves, a frisbee across the sky.

On the school roof, the wind-gauge whirls.
Jeans and t-shirts are flytin on the washing-line.

A peerie moustache
whips up on the ferry's prow.

The world is turning,
                tuning to the wind.

ii. Slow Air

The wind from faraway Iceland drives the swell
beneath our feet as the Hendra lifts.
O my God! It's the Stoor Worm yawning.

The wind takes a deep breath from its diaphragm,
        exhales
                through the hollow aluminium rails.

The wind slides and slurs,
        flicking
                the grass seeds with grace notes.

The wind dirls on the drystane wall,
        whispers
                or hums through the cracks.

iii. Skeklers' Reel

Midnight titters, scuffles at the door.
It dares you to open:
the joke's on you.

Batten down your roofs!
Net down your rubbish bags!
Pebbles on the peat shed,
driving hail of showers.

Up, down,
            turn around.
Hold onto your heads!

Veering up the voe, swirling round the salmon-rings,
ripping out the mussel strings,
skerry-skooshing,
        toft-tearing,
                rock-wrenching gale.

A fat lady in a helmet
        and bronze cones for breasts
                hits the high A.

                All hell-get-out.

        Arms wide embrace the world.

THE NJUGGLE

At midnight on Hallowe'en, my back to the moon,
I looked in the mirror to scry my lover-to-be.
His face rose like a drowned man's.

At twilight I walked by the lochan in the hills
where the whaap's cry wavers from the reeds.
A piebald pony ambled up. His nostrils

pulsed as he blew into my hand.
Clicking my tongue, I patted his flanks
and his muscles shivered like water in the wind.

When he lowered his head, I knew I must mount.
I rode him through the night, gripping his back
between my thighs till I slid on our sweat

and he rolled me into cold, green fire.
I clung to his mane blooming with algae,
his shoulders encrusted with mussels and mire.

His hooves softened and opened into a fan
of fingers and toes. Belly flattening, spine
whip-lashing, he bucked and shrank into a man.

As the dark fled, he turned to plunge me under
but dawn broke and he poured through my arms.
I was alone, calling, calling with no answer,

only the widening circles on the loch.

MY LOVE, THE SHETLAND TROWIE

His eyes are like extinguished lighthouses
His eyebrows are a gadderie of fiddlers
His nose a broken sea-arch
His jaw is like the blue ramp of the ferry lowering
then clanking shut
His mouth a hollow gloup
His teeth smashed Blue Vodka bottles
His saliva is like the seven tides of Shetland
His chest hair a scratchy kishie
His arms whirling wind turbines
His elbows are like crane-winches
His legs are posts bristling with barnacles
His buttocks are half-submerged skerries
His member is like the seal's head bobbing up
and down in the harbour
His bollocks are ponies' nose-bags
His pubic hair is the hay-nets flung
over plastic rubbish bags
His arsehole is like the slippery steps down
to the lower deck
His urine is the swell in a Force 10 gale
His sweat is salty houb water
His oxters are like skories' nests
His nipples are the rings of salmon-traps
His navel is a fire-bucket peppered
with fag butts
His skin is like stiff, sea-drenched gaiters
His breath's a blow-hole
His sigh the haar
His fart is like the flare at Sullom Voe

THE CHILD OF BRECKON SANDS
(Isle of Yell)

My peerie boy, the only voices you hear
are mine, the shalder shaking loose his cry
and the red-throated rain-goose:

a' wet, wet, wet,
waur wadder, waur wadder.

You stumble, lurch, drag your feet on land
but slipping into water, you circle like silk.
Far from gossip, we gather tongues of kelp
bursting with flies.

When I wake in black winter
to the song of the seals I remember the cave
and the sea-lashed rock
where you were born.

I gaze into your eyes, blank as milk.
You do not understand a word I say.
Fatherless boy, who will look after you
when I am dead?

SHAELA

I'm knitting a shawl of light summer mist.
More air than wool, it can slip through a wedding ring.

I will hap up my bairn when he suckles at night,
at the dead time when the world's asleep

and it's only me and him and the moon
and the crying of the seals

circling, sliding over and under,
over and under, snout to tail

until it's hard to tell
which one is which.

What is me and what is my bairn,
my moon-gazer who fell from the stars?

DE'IL TAK THE MINISTER
(Fetlar)

Cut with voes, worn out at the elbows,
a thin place
        where the spits of land rise like whales from the haar,
        where a nun prays, solitary but brimful with laughter,
        where by mid-day, the reds of the buoys are eye-popping,
the blue of the ferry is more intense than blue has ever been.

Before you know it, there are only two children in the school,
and next there'll be no school, no hall, no church, no pub,

only the wind, the white cross of the gannet's plunge.
Light all summer, dark all winter

when trowies may lure you into their hills
        for a night of jigs and slip-jigs, strathspeys and reels
        and you'll emerge a hundred years later
        to find your friends and family are dust.

PAGANINI'S FIDDLE IN A SHETLAND BARN
(Trondra)

Crofter, boat-builder and fiddle-maker,
Tommy lifts his fiddle and sound falls:
water lapping in freshwater lochs.
He sways and its hull flames silver or dark.

Its back is figured maple, taking the strain.
A spruce deck flexes with the swell.
Its C-curves are stream-lined, ocean-going.
The strings are halyards vibrating in the winds.

Heading down the voe, out to the Far Haaf,
the fiddle responds to the hand of a helmsman
who understands local waters: skerries, roosts
rip-tides and deep-sea storms.

DA SLOCKIT LIGHT

the wind
flings

the islands

too far and wide

for the eye to scan

scattering shadows
scattering folk

only two or three crofts still showing a light

as night falls

AYRE

(Tombola, St Ninian's Isle)

Airy and eerie:
a stretch of pebbles, a peninsula,
where the opera of the tide is ever
answering, echoing
gesture with gesture,
breath with breath,
ecstatic airs
from elsewhere.

UNST
i. Ultima Thule (Hermaness)

You would think it's so remote
that here you'd find peace.

Mist, the breath of bewitched Herma,
rises from the moor.

The only way-markers are wooden planks
laid over the squelch and suck of bog.

I pause, afraid of bonxies,
shadows lifting out of the peat.

How much further north must I go
to find a song so sweet that I plunge

into its icy waters, forgetting
I cannot swim?

ii. Steekit Stimna

In a land stripped of trees,
there are no distractions.

Only the intense blue
of lochs, the long voes,
skies so pale they are transparent.

Mocked by yellow fog,
its damp cloth, tasting of metal,
pressing against my face,
I can hardly breathe.

My mind fills with water beetles,
sphagnum moss and peaty pools:
all I can see.

The further north I go, the more
I must face myself.

iii. Keen of Hamar

To fear the edge,
invisible in the mist,
straining to hear the footfalls of waves.

To lose my way
in a serpentine path over Ice Age scree,
still shifting.

To hunch, inch by inch,
over a scattering of pebbles
through a telescope of finger and thumb.

To see a galaxy
of frog orchids, mouse ears,
moonwort, sandwort, sea plantain.

To stare, like a child.
No playmates. Eyes down.

vi. Hyperborea

Muckle Flugga,
flashes intermittent hosannas,
its unmanned hopes for man.

Light hides itself in dark:
Lucky Minny's Oo fluttering in the bog,
white suns in burnt heather.

Pray for those lost at sea
when waves become mountains
toppling onto the lighthouse rock,
when spray, higher than the tower,
is thunder and smoke

and the poverty wind blows.

v. Muckle Flugga

Mist, mist, drizzle.
The surprise of blue.

The *Julie Rose* passes through mist
to snow in summer,
a wedding day of wings.

Cliffs swirl in puffin clouds.
Fulmars trust to unseen thermals.
Gannets cross-stitch the sky.

As we near the Rumblings,
dazzling with guano, we are assaulted
by cracked bells, an *exultate domine.*

If I came for solitude,
this is not the place.

vi. Da Mirrie Dancers

The skies rip open:
aurora borealis.
Fox-fire brushes the mountains.

I keep silent, in case light-storms
tangle in my hair.
Perhaps I'll whistle, if I dare,
to bring them closer.

Green light rustles.
It's the footsteps of the dead
from the world beyond the wind.

Unfolding, shimmering across the skies,
it fades to red.

My compass is warped.

vii. A Visitation

A spraint, a paw-print
in kelp-strewn sand.
These were my only sightings.

I kept watch at Baltasound
for shadows rippling across the road
from salt-water to fresh.

I waited every evening,
for the underside of waves
to turn into undulating fur.

On the last day,
when I had stopped searching,
he rose up from the sea.

Slicked with dreadlocks,
he stared me out.

viii. Unst

You should come by sea,
like the early saints
and pass through the Blue Mull,
deep whale-road.

Though I saw neither the minke whale
(so momentary a glimpse
you think you imagined it)

nor the humpback breaching
obscured in spray,
I know they were there.

I saw the skull of a porpoise,
the blank socket of its eye.

Like Thomas,
I put my hand in the cavity.

WHAT MUST NOT BE SPOKEN ON WATER

Peering into the water the line man
sees light in the chimney.
We haul in silence another white, and another.

When the glider sets and the gloamer rises,
we'll set the cloot and steer
by the blessed house of the upstander

back to the helpmate, feeding
scraps to the hirki, milking the boorik.
At last she'll light the bright one.

The light-footed, playful one, the wailer
will see off the bone-biter, then wash
her own face and dab behind her ears.

NIGHT FALLS
(Mousa Broch)

Not a murmuration
but single pieces of night
slip from the sky: stormy petrels

flickering over the stony beach,
disappearing into the dark
between boulders.

A churring, ratching
of thousands of keys turning in clockwork
reverberates in the cage of my chest.

The whole island vibrates.
At the broch, I place my ear to its drystone walls
and hear it breathe.

FIRST LONG WALK AFTER CONVALESCENCE
(Fair Isle)

The blue cross on the Sumburgh plane
is stretched in the wind.
Skylarks are drilling holes in the sky.

An irritation of midges
and the hazy static of bog-cotton
blur the Dunlins Sink.

The Burn of Fursie is shrunk
to a slit in the bog, pock-marked
by water-beetles balanced on prongs.

Hovering, like a brown mote
in the corner of an eye: the bonxie—
a dislocated shadow.

The valley opens in a shock
of raw light, cumulae billowing,
the ack-ack of gulls.

At each step, a further juddering view:
the Peerie, the Muckle,
the Mid Heads o' Yesness.

But no views of geos, or caves.
The Wirvie: nothing but sheep turds,
rabbit droppings, scrag heather.

No spectacular blow-hole spoutings.
No churning voices
from the Kirn o' Skroo.

Only the yellow algae on Golden Water
shining a fools' blessing.
Ahead, the North Lighthouse—

and below, O Stack,
Peerie O Stack,
the jagged fins of the Slithers.

WIND DOG

A half-bitten smile,
a hesitant kiss,
a hand let slip

—*Windoge, vindauga*, wind-eye:
the wind is not content
only to have a voice.

Without sun,
without rain,
it cannot see or be seen.

Not a black hole
into which everything
is sucked, but an iris

flexing.

FLOUT

I must learn to tease,
pull gently,

let loose
any dirt or flecks of peat.

Comb to remove naps or bumps.
Leave long fibres (best for fine spinning).

Turn

and comb in another direction
until I have a square.

Why do I always expect it to be easy,
to come out pure first time?

If too dry,
a little oil is allowed.

Glossary

birl	– whirl
bonxie	– great skua
dirl	– vibrate
Far Haaf	– deep-sea ocean fishing, beyond coastal waters
flout	– square of wool prepared for spinning.
geo	– a narrow chasm, often ending in a cliff falling at right angles to a beach
gloup	– collapsed cave
haar	– sea-mist
houb	– salty loch
kishie	– woven straw pannier
oo	– wool (Lucky Minny's Oo is bog-cotton)
oxter	– arm-pit
peerie	– little
rain-goose	– red-throated diver
rant	– tune
roosts	– tidal-races
shaela	– a light summer mist, grey in colour
shalder	– oyster-catcher
skorie	– adolescent herring gull
slockit	– put out or extinguished
steekit stimna	– dense fog
trow or *trowie*	– Shetland troll or goblin
waur wadder	– worse weather
whaap	– curlew

Author's note: I am not a Shetlandic (Shaetlan) speaker. I have picked up words from my visits there and am also indebted to *The Shetland Dictionary* by John J Graham (*The Shetland Times*, 1979, revised 2009), although sometimes I use a more current spelling.

Notes

The Wind's Rant, p. 6
Stoor Worm: a Norse/Shetlandic mythic water-dragon. Skeklers: guizers dressed in straw costumes at Hallowe'en or Auld Year's Night who performed wild dances and mischievous tricks.

The Njuggle, p. 8
The Njuggle is a demon water horse or pony found in Shetland and Orkney folklore.

Da Slockit Light, p. 14
The title of a tune by Tom Anderson who revived traditional fiddle playing in Shetland. The poem was inspired by listening to it played in tribute to him at his grave by visiting musicians on the 'Fiddle Frenzy' course.

Keen of Hamar, p. 18
This harsh landscape, now a nature reserve on the Isle of Unst, is of great geological and botanical interest with its rare, mostly tiny, flowers, especially the Edmonston Chickweed locally known as 'mouse ear', discovered in 1837 by Thomas Edmonston aged 12.

Da Mirrie Dancers, p. 21
This Shetlandic phrase means 'the Merry Dancers', which are the *aurora borealis* or Northern Lights.

What Must Not Be Spoken on Water p. 24
It was considered unlucky to speak too directly whilst at sea, hence *cloot* ('a cloth'—a sail) and the invented words *boorik*—cow, and *hirki*—pig.

Wind Dog, p. 28
'Wind Dog' is Scots for a broken rainbow.